THEN & NOW

SHEFFIELD

Vol 1

Hillsborough, Langsett, Kelvin
Malin Bridge, Neepsend, St. Philips,
Wardsend, Wadsley Bridge

For George and Dora Clayton

Ron Clayton
Made in Sheffield since 1952

Acknowledgements:

I would like to thank:

Mrs Cowley and other Sheffield Education Home Tutors, Charlie Haydock, Gordon Hodgkinson, AW Goodfellow (Wisewood Secondary School) Septimus Henry Ward, Henderson and his Relish, the Immortal Ron Springett.

Local studies Library, Surrey Street, who have provided many pictures in this book. All images with a reference number on bottom right of the photo are on their website: www.**picturesheffield**.co.uk

Copies of pictures may be ordered online.

Ron Clayton was conceived some time before the 11th August 1952

Allergic to fish, he is the youngest son of the late George Clayton, Fishmonger And Licenced Dealer In Game. His father once looked at Ron's feet and said "Tha'd make a good copper thee' but Ron was too soft and spent many years subsequently wondering what he could have been, before realising his true vocation, that of a "Professional Sheffielder."

Like all Sheffielders, he loves his city with a passion but remains bemused as to how the city can have demolished so many of its historic buildings yet wax lyrical over Park Hill Flats. A lapsed Wednesdayite ['They don't come and see me when I'm bad] but being a Sheffielder, has a respect for the red and white half of the city. A lover of South Yorkshire in general, he gets a skin rash anywhere south of Chesterfield.

Like many of his generation he is convinced that the world has gone mad, deplores the disappearance of proper nurses' uniforms, Wadsley Village, Wards Fine Malt Ales and the rise of boxer shorts and has a fondness for Kipling ['Mr Kipling makes exceedingly good poems'] and a mania for the Rolling Stones while Cher sliding down a gun barrel or dancing on a bar has been known to bring him out in a hot flush..

Ron's particular Sheffield historical interests are Sheffield's Castle, Charlie Peace, Hillsborough Barracks, The Manor Lodge and interesting gravestone inscriptions. [For a more comprehensive list of his 'Historical Talks, Walks And Entertainments' see inside backpage].

One of those dwindling bunch of Sheffielders who live and die in the same post code area, he has lived in S6 for most of his life. Before he goes to that Great North Stand in the sky he has five remaining ambitions.

To show folk round the remains of Sheffield Castle, to get some more sun on his ageing bones, to own a Jack Russell Terrier called Enoch and get into a pair of Wrangler Jeans.

Foreward/Preface

S6 is the place I've miss-spent most of my S6 Years. I suspect I'll get carried out of it in a box on my way to the pilot light at the 'Crem de la Crem' at Grenoside (or Genoside as Jack Bell used to say). My ashes will end up in S6 (but not on the Wednesday ground.)

It's a place intersected by fast flowing streams on which Sheffield's steel industry was founded, bounded by moors, heathland, leafy valleys and the Peak National Park, all rich with wildlife (bit like Hillsborough Corner on Friday/Saturday night), home to the football team that has broke my heart more then any woman, to one of the few remaining walled barracks in the UK, a park that has some of the features of an original 18th Century gentlemen's residence. Its the legendary birth place of Robin of Loxley, or Robin Hood as he's better known, where a murderer was gibbetted, cutlers produced their wares, body snatchers resided or practised. A place where you can still follow the packhorse routes, roll back time to the great inundation of 1864, see the finest motte and bailey castle in South Yorkshire and the work of a minister turned(none too successfully) businessman and builder, visit mysterious earthworks, stone circles and find real pubs for real people.

At Bradfield and Ecclesfield there are 15th century churches, at Stannington you can learn of a Roman Auxiliary Soldier's discharge diplomas. There is Neepsend where blanco was made and Wards End where Bassetts Liquorice Allsorts still are. Rich in industrial archaeology and walks and scenic views and fresh air.

It's a place of ghosts and out of the way graveyards, of legendary pubs and landlords, pork sandwiches to die for, Co-op Sunday breakfasts, the best greasy spoon in Sheffield, a walled garden, Rivelin & Loxley valleys and Wadsley and Loxley Commons.

And now it's being dragged kicking and screaming (like Hillsborough Corner on Friday and Saturday nights) into the 21st Century. Sixer's are being civilised as the young professionals move in because they can't afford Crookes. Stand by as they put wall paper on the wheelie bins, buy composters and have Sainsbury's deliver their groceries (We've even got a Lounge Lizard or two on Holme Lane) What follows is a cornucopia of my bit of Sheffield, S6 past and present, here and there. Enjoy it and come for a walk with me round Hillsborough Barracks or up Loxley Bottoms in search of Robin Hood.

Ron Clayton
Writer in Residence, New Barrack Tavern,
1996-2008
May 2008

Looking Towards S6, Kelvin top left, with Royal Infirmary in front, St Philips centre right and Neepsend top right.

S22113

Neepsend Power Station

Well should we have kept our cooling towers as 'Iconic Structures?' The ones at Tinsley are doomed like their opposite numbers at Neepsend. These cooling towers were part of Neepsend Power Station.

Crookes Valley Recreation Ground

Trucks belonging to the barrage balloon party, the truck in the middle of the picture is the winch truck, complete with gas trailor. The soldiers appear to be laying out ballast bags of sand. Norton was their base, which remained in RAF use until 1965.

Pondersosa

Barrage ballon being inspected by the curious Sheffielders in same way the first planes to Sheffield's short lived airport were.

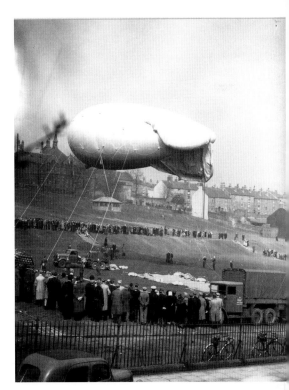

Multi coloured Nether Thorpe High Rise Flats. (ooops sorry, apartments)

This is where Sheffield author and St Luke's Hospice fund-raiser, the late Fred Pass was born and grew up. His books, 'Weerz me Dad?' and 'Weerz me Mam?' give a fascinating insight into life in this area in the 1940s and 50s just before the area was re-developed in the 1960s.

The Infirmary

Note the roundhouse in the left foreground, original (1797) block on the right, haunted by the 'Grey Lady'. Some of the early photos of the outpatients department show a lot of men and boys with eye patches due to injuries caused by grinding. I always remember the lifts and visiting Dr Sneddon. Sadly a pretty inaccessible part of Sheffield's heritage these days.

Upperthorpe Baths and Library

Not much altered to view, but much changed since Aunt Delina and Uncle Tots used to keep the Meadow Street Hotel and Aunt Ada lived on Daniel Hill Street. Built in 1879 to alleviate the poor conditions of the folk who lived in the area, not far away the home of Montgomery, the hymn worker, not the Field Marshall.

Don Brewery – St Philip's

Imagine the Sheffield Flood sweeping through here in 1864! The Don Brewery sign, or one of them, has been embellished on the reverse of the wall to the front of the Globe Works. Now one of the 'Jewels In The Crown' of the new Sheffield.

St Philip's Church

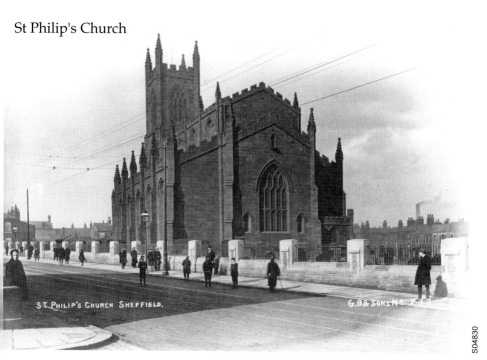

The first burial in St Philip's Church yard was 1825, that of a brick maker, and is preserved in Morrisons Wall. The story goes that the clock on the tower of St Philip's was illuminated so it would shine on Wards end Cemetery to deter grave robbers. Load of Cobblers to be honest.

St Philip's Church

Bombed during the Blitz. Two disinterments to remove bodies for road widening were carried out 1966-70 with the site fenced off from view. However, the fencing was not high enough to prevent us Central Technical School-bound kids looking down from the top deck of a double decker.

Now bushes catch wind-swept carrier bags. Intimately connected with the Wardsend Cemetery 'Grave Robbery' incident.

The Globe Works

S09916

A rare view of the Globe Works with St Philip's gravestones standing upright in the foreground. Following the refurbishment of the Globe Works in the late 1980s there was a short lived pub called the Rattener's Rest on the ground floor.

The Globe Works with it's classical frontage being perhaps the first purpose cutlery factory, circa 1818. Damaged in the Great Inundation of 1864 when they belonged to one Mr Ibbotson. Derelict in 1970s, a lovely bit of Old Sheffield Town.

Blanchards on the right hand side. One of the household names in Sheffield along with Wilson Tupholmes, Wigfalls, Bowaters, Blaskeys. Hungry Wolf's 'Meat and Tater pie' is recommended along with Rosis and that butchers on the corner of Sharrow Vale Road. Don't forget Henderson's Relish.

Gilpin Street

The Art Deco garage on the left has recently been demolished for, yes, apartments. In the distance, Parkwood Springs and land that the council once did not know who it belonged to. The Duke of Norfolk?

Langsett Road and the Sally Army *"Will you come to the mission, will you come, there's a free cup of tea and a bun"*. Steptoe and Son, immortal, unlike Ant and Dec.

S17515

The Hillsborough Hotel on the left in a view that has not much changed. Probably less traffic. The original name of the pub, The Hero And His Horse, was a reference to Wellington and his steed at Waterloo (Copenhagen). It then became the Wellington and was run by Geoff Cook, Wednesdayite. Del Tilling refurbished it and it is now a popular venue on the Real Ale Circuit. Nice nosh too. Now owned by Helen and Andrew Walker.

Langsett Road, fire engine from Division Street or West Bar? Where's the crew? The Shop nearest the Hillsborough Hotel is Mick Flynn's Motorcycle dismantler.

Wood Street

Distant view of Farfield (Formerly Muffin, the Owl). The gasometer looks lovely by moonlight. Original entrance to the Wellington/Hillsborough Hotel was in between the traffic light and no entry sign on the lower photograph.

Flora Street, named after someone's female relative. This was the site of the first Sheffield Barracks which was much smaller than the one built later at Hillsborough.

Kelvin

The only remaining reproduceable photograph of the 1795 Kelvin or Horse Barracks. This shows the hospital converted into tenements.

An interesting view of a pre-Kelvin Kelvin, There is a grainy film of the Kelvin being built. Nowadays the name of Philadelphia is used especially when the Philadelphia Beer and Music Festival is in full swing.

Burgoyne Road 'nick' is on the left hand side. The police station was formerly Flint's dentist and is now, guess what, student accommodation. Thompson's dentist on the other side. Note security shutters these days to stop folk pinching dental floss.

On the way to Bamforth Street. Bamforth was an important landowner in 18th Century Sheffield and owned Wadsley Hall.

Langsett Road on the right hand side is the Lyceum Hotel where Lewis met his assailant. Cuthbert Bank on the left in both pictures. Further up from the Cuthbert are some pigeon lofts. Surprised the council hasn't listed them. Quite ingenious in the way they are constructed but some might say they give the wrong impression for a European City. Perhaps they are 'iconic' though.

Hillsborough Barracks

The officers quarters. Mixture of Gothic and Castellated architecture. Note the impressive railings that weren't pinched for the war effort in 1939 – 1945. Same as Buckingham Palace.

Again two versions of the tram. Bottom left is the Art Noveau former soldiers home now the 393 club. Below that the Queens ground with a lovely SH Ward piece of stained glass. A lovely Wards House when Fred Kelsey had it. Note the street name on the gas lamp. You are looking down what was known as Barrack Hill. Many will also remember Reg and Rose Hydes who used to have a greengrocer's at the top of Dykes Hall Road.

Hillsborough Barracks

S17574

On Guard. The gate could tell a tale or two. I came across the oldest photo of the Barracks some years ago. One for Volume 2.

Hillsborough Barracks

Note the band and the variation in height of the drummer boys. Reminiscent of opening/finishing sequences of Blackadder Goes Forth!
"Busy, Busy, Busy, Eyes right, pick up that shopping trolley you orrible little man!"

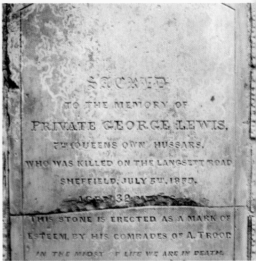

The gravestones of 3 military men and a railway navigator or 'navvie', 2 of whom died violently. The gravestones of the military men are from the Kelvin or Horse Barracks – not Hillsborough. Lewis was stabbed to death by a drunken civilian and Kidd was crushed by a railway engine. Note the doggerel verse. I rescued these with the help of a chap from the council, the John Brunton Partnership of Architects and George Longden builders. They were originally in St Philips Church Graveyard and are now in Morrisons. Look out for more of these in Volume 2.

Wadsley Lane/Middlewood Road

Junction of Wadsley Lane/Middlewood Road with tramtracks in both images. Nowadays this area is a Mecca for hungry S6's with Beres Pork Sandwiches a particular gastronomic delight. Remember the Chinese laundry and Atkinsons pie shop?

Hillsborough Corner

The Old Blue Ball after the Great Flood of 1864. Taken from Walkley Lane from a position adjacent to the Masons Arms. Hillsborough Bridge is intact in the foreground. Is this incorporated in the later structure? Note the damage to the Hillsborough Inn, left hand side, the floorboards were lifted up by the force of the inundation. Note the island on the river recently caused by the flood of 2007.

Hillsborough Corner

A rather cramped view of Hillsborough Corner but one with more character than it's successor below. Leg Ends as it's known locally, was formerly Timpsons. Bought one or two pairs of desert boots there in me time.

Hillsborough Corner, again with two generations of trams. The locals gawping at the photographer would now be in Leg Ends Sports Bar, peering over the bridge, shopping or going int' betting shop. Subway used to be Burton where you could purchase 'cavalier' flared slacks.   Usual Burton foundation stone.

Hillsborough Corner

S16304

The Hillsborough Inn, closed 1960, is a massive building. Some of the officers from the Hillsborough Garrison took their meals there in the second half of the 19th Century and the story goes they would amuse themselves by throwing hot pennies to the local kids. These days they'd probably get a traffic cone back in return.

Old cottage with outbuildings in the shadow of Regent Court Flats. Taken on a washday before the days of fabric conditioners? Would have been caked in mud, and worse, by the 1864 flood. Below, Swan Morton's on the left.

Neepsend

The Farfield Inn, Neepsend pictured after the Great Flood of 1867. Note the destroyed bridge in the foreground. In the lesser inundation of June 2007 water actually reached the front door of this 1754 Georgian Gentleman's residence and listed building. It's largely unchanged today apart from the pub frontage on the ground floor elevation. In recent years it's been a lodging house complete with resident white Ford Cortina. One day I hope to see a Sheffield Flood trail plaque affixed to the wall. Club Mill Road to the left hand side is currently a haven for fly tippers.

Local kids, one with a football ? On the right hand side is the Loxley/Rivelin before it meets the Don. In the background is Swift Brothers Rolling Mill. This stretch of the river is home to the occasional B&Q shopping trolley.

Penistone Road

Junction of Penistone Road and Parkside Road. Bottom lodge of Hillsborough Park on right hand side. Houses on left all now gone. Not much traffic about, taken on a Sunday morning – early?

Penistone Road/Beulah Road

In those days you could leave your bike unattended without having to put two locks, of at least £60 on it. Possibly someone watching over it on the right. They don't seem to have cleared the drains in those days either. Beulah is a female name and in Hebrew means 'married'. Rather Hawaiian/Polynesian influenced sports centre below.

Wardsend

The Five Arches when rural, before the Southey Estate was built. Wardsend Cottages to the left. Some adventurous folk have painted slogans on the parapet over the years.

Malin Bridge

Stannington Road, bottom, before it joins Malin Bridge (Loxley Bottoms really, it sounds better in the estate agents brochure). German Wilson's cornmill on the left.

The mill is recently being refurbished after being derelict for ten plus years. It's being turned into bijou apartments where you can sit and watch the tyres in the river.

Loxley Valley/Malin Bridge

LOXLEY VALLEY SHEFFIELD·

Still industrial in parts then. Very much residential these days. Taken from Walkley Bank, allotments in the foreground. What a skyline! Loxley and Wadsley Commons. One of my boyhood haunts. Big rock, crags, Bower Cottage, etc.

Mouse Hole Forge

What a rugged landscape it was once. Owned by John and Julia Hatfield. They wrote the seminal work on Samuel Bolsover and Old Sheffield Plate.

Penistone Road/Leppings Lane

Note the cantilever North Stand of Sheffield Wednesday FC. The team guaranteed to snatch defeat from victory to misquote Uncle Bill Slim, hero of the forgotten 14th Army. Spent many a miss-spent hour of my youth in the former 'Wembley of The North'. A long time since it was called that!

The group on the left look as if they are a bit chilly. The gentleman with the moustache is presumably the owner and has refused to sell the chabby any Pantatella's.

Wadsley Bridge

An 'old' Gate Pub. Tram on the way and a 'Ford Pop' in the other direction. And a 'New' Gate Pub. For a photo of the old Gate in greater detail see volume 2. Note the road widening.

Dial House

Dial House, built in 1804 by French Napoleonic Prisoners of War. Probably ordered their baguettes from Dora Websters, in Catch Bar Lane. It was formerly a gentleman's private residence.

Note the sundial by Coopland over the door. Top picture indicates how narrow Ben Lane was. Up past the club was Jack Beckworth's grocers. A real character, his carpet slippers and brown smock and battalions of dead flies on the fly paper.

Dial House is in the distance in this view up towards Ben Lane, Wadsley. The newly completed Sutton Estate is on the right. In the mid-ground are the predecessors of today's Street Force *(minus high vis jackets)* and some villagers. The site is occupied today by a variety of shops but is so run down since Mr Nicholson the cobbler, Mr Hopkinson the Hairdresser, Mrs Beckworth (wife of Jack Beckworth, shopkeeper in Ben Lane) and Mrs Marsh used to be here.

Wadsley Bridge

Says's it all doesn't it? Oh Doctor Beeching was that the right prescription?

Wadsley Bridge, Old Bridge

On the right the Travellers, much altered but with a late 17th Century date over a fireplace.

Loxley House

This interesting old house has had a chequered history and would welcome the attention of a 'house detective'. Originally built by Thomas Halliday there are later additions by Payne. It has been a private dwelling, a refuge for Belgian refugees from the Great War, a cripples' home and the TS Sheffield for Sheffield Sea Cadets. Dr Payne is buried in the grounds following a tiff with a former Vicar of Wadsley.

The good doctor told the curate he'd never enter his church. The man of the cloth reckoned he'd have the last say but said Doctor won in the end. Dr Payne's universal panacea for all ills was a hot blanket - just think how much dosh this would save the NHS. The figure head on the right was a common sight in the sixties and has the figure head of a 19th Century Royal Monitor or Gunboat. They were used in shallow water to hunt down pirates and slaves and anyone who tried to break the Pax Britannica. A sea cadet petty officer told the cadets 'to lose it' so they burnt it! Haunted by an Irish ghost called 'Mick'. In front of the house there was a World War II 40mm Bofors anti-aircraft gun. There was a very interesting licensed bar. Reminiscent of when we had a navy, the way things are going we'll be hard pressed to enforce Pax Britannica on Dam Flask soon! The Sea Cadets were normally a well behaved lot, however there was the occasional snowball lobbed against the windows of Ben Lane as they made their way home after parade. Famous plot to pinch the Cadet's 303s/.22 rifles in the sixties.

The remains of the original wall above can be seen below. Pretty boring scene then and the same today. The Gilders showroom has recently been rebuilt. The trams went and came back! Hank Hooper, Wednesday FA winner in 1935 had a tobacconists further down the road on the right hand side.

The Lost Village of Wadsley

The usual view of Old Wadsley that you see. The Horse and Jockey pub alone survives today. One of two traditional sites of the village green is shown on the left and has been recently built upon. At the time of printing the pub is closed. Locally famous landlord/landlady couple Bob and Lorraine Sabine are still at the Masons on Langsett Road. Later it was Henry and Murie, from Pitsmoor.

The Lost Village of Wadsley

A typical old Wadsleyite, flat capped hat and fiercely in-dependent. They don't make them like that these days. Who was he I wonder? Note the whitewashed cottage wall. Off for a pint of Tetleys in the Star? Jim Pulfrey being the landlord at the time.

A grand old couple from the last days of Wadsley village. One of the reasons they pulled down Wadsley was the unhealthy living conditions and the fact they only had one door! Note the lady's pinny.

The living conditions, whilst not 'Rose Cottage', don't seem to have shortened the lives of Darby and Joan. I would love to hear from their family!

The Lost Village of Wadsley

The rather substantial house on the left was once the residence of one of our local clowns. Whose name, like my hair, has escaped me. Never mind, saved me a fortune in combs.

The Lost Village of Wadsley

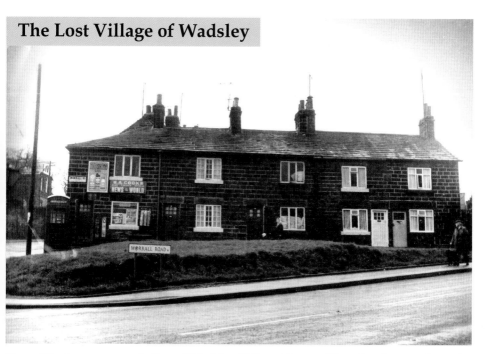

One of the two supposed sites of Wadsley Village Green. The other being where the houses are which replaced the above. They were supposedly built to the same line as their predecessors after some of us S6s raised the issue. There was an alledged tunnel from the old manor house to the telephone box.

Wadsley Manor House

The original Wadsley Manor House stood where the flats are in Laird Road. It had a massive key to the front door which I haven't seen for years. I know of only three illustrations, the best one in the Rev. H Kirk Smith's history of Wadsley, the parish to whom he ministered and obviously loved. The above shows the front elevation facing onto Laird Road from a 19th Century drawing. The view below is taken from the right side of the old house. A sad loss, one of many of Sheffields historic buildings.

Ron Clayton is a professional Sheffielder, Wit and Raconteur (whatever the latter means) and plays mean and menacing *Sam Garvin* when called upon.

He gives talks or local historical entertainments to a diverse range of audiences such as *Sheffield Rotary, The Norton Association For The Prosecution Of Felons, Wise Old Owls, The Senior Blades,* and is a regular contributor to Sheffield's highly regarded *Off The Shelf Festival,* as well as writing acerbic letters to the Sheffield press. He used to be on *Radio Sheffield* and has written for the *Sheffield Sixer* and the *Hillsborough Gazette,* as well as doing the *Sheffield Castle Invisible Tour* for *Sheffield Environment Weeks* during Spring, Summer and Autumn. He does these on a Sunday (12-2, meet outside Sheffield Cathedral) but is available on other days or evenings given sufficient notice. Look out for his leaflet in the *Sheffield Tourism Office* on Norfolk Row, *Sheffield Scene* on Surrey Street and *Civic Information/Local Studies Central Library* on Surrey Street, or call him on 0114 234 6669.

He comes highly recommended;

"He was great fun" - Sheffield Family History Society.

"Everyone had a good time" - Crystal Peaks Library.

"Could listen to him for hours" - Friends of Wisewood School.

Subjects include - Sheffield Castle, The Inside Story; Harvey Teasdale And Other Sheffield Barmpots; Charlie Peace, His Lives, Crimes and Loves; Privy Tales, Stories Of Famous Sheffield Toilets; Up Loxley Bottoms, In Search of Robin Hood; The Bar Maid's Apron, A Look At Sheffield's Vanishing Pub Heritage; A Fishmonger's Lad Growing Up In S6 and S10 in the 50s, 60s and 70s, and many others. His guided walks around Historical Sheffield are highly regarded by those who have been on them. Join him on the new Drinking Man's/Woman's Sheffield Flood Trail Walk. (Bring some money).

A few more of our titles you may enjoy:

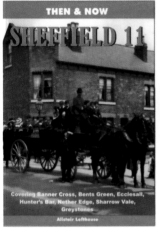 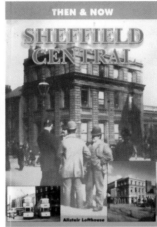 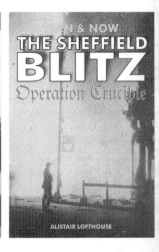

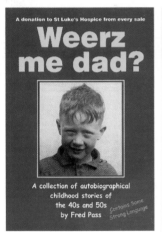  

available in all good bookshops or online at:

www.printanddesignshop.co.uk